*For the endangered ecosystems across our land
and for our national parks
and to the children who are helping to save them
—J.C.G.*

*To Marjory Stoneman Douglas,
whose pioneering spirit
helped preserve what remains of the River of Grass
—W.M.*

# JEAN CRAIGHEAD GEORGE
# EVERGLADES

HarperCollins*Publishers*

# PAINTINGS BY WENDELL MINOR

The storyteller poled the children under arching trees into a sunny water glade. He sat down and leaned toward them.

"I am going to tell you a story," he said. "It is not a story about a person or a mythical creature. It is not even a story about an animal."

The children looked at each other and waited.

"It's a story about a river." He swung his arms in a wide circle. "This river, the miraculous Everglades of Florida.

"My story will be different from any you have heard, because this river is like no other river on Earth. There is only one Everglades."

The children leaned forward. He began.

First there was sunshine on a blue-green sea.

It was the Age of the Seashells.

The seashells formed a rock called limestone on the sea bottom. Over the eons the sea lowered, and the rock became land. The long Florida peninsula took shape in warm, sunny waters.

Purple clouds, flashing with lightning, roiled and boomed above the land. Rain gushed from the storm clouds in summer. Sun bathed the land in winter. Moss grew, then ferns, then grass and trees.

The rain eroded holes in the soft limestone and filled them with water. Florida glistened with green land and blue-green lakes.

One was Lake Okeechobee, round, deep, and as clear as window glass.

Lake Okeechobee filled to its brim and spilled over. The spill became a river that seeped one hundred miles down the peninsula from Lake Okeechobee to the Florida Bay. It was fifty miles wide and only six inches deep in most places.

This river did not chortle and splash. It did not crash over falls and race. It was a slow river that gleamed like quicksilver. We know it today as the Everglades.

Into the shallow, warm river came tiny one-celled animals and plants. They lived and died and made gray-green soil on the bottom of the river. Saw grass took root in the soil.

The grass prospered. When the winds blew, the saw grass clattered like a trillion swords. Each sword was edged with cutting spines. Of the larger animals, only the leathery alligator could walk unharmed among the terrible spears of the saw grass.

Around the stems of the grass scurried the young of insects, and tiny crabs and snails. Little fish found these to be excellent eating. Turtles and alligators found the fish to be excellent eating. Every wild thing ate well, and there was still an enormous abundance.

To the abundance came the birds. Clouds of lacy, white egrets made their home in the Everglades.

Every day a blizzard of wood storks dropped into the grass and dined on the snails, crabs, bugs, and fish.

A profusion of pink flamingos hunted in the shallow mudflats.

Hundreds of miles of roseate spoonbills vacuumed the ponds and shallows with their sievelike bills.

A myriad of little songbirds fluttered through the trees that grew on the islands in the river of saw grass.

Quantities of alligators roamed the grass and dug pools for their young. Into their pools came fish and turtles, herons and anhingas, and billions of frogs, snakes, and snails.

A multitude of panthers, raccoons, deer, and otter came to the river. They made their homes on the beautiful islands.

A plenitude of orchids bloomed and turned the island trees into colorful cathedral windows.

A plethora of lizards and anoles clambered over the orchids, and two thousand kinds of plants, including palms, vines, bushes, grasses, and trees.

When all were in place, the Everglades was a living kaleidoscope of color and beauty. It glittered with orchids, grass, trees, birds, panthers, raccoons, snakes, mosquitoes, fish—all things large and small that make the Earth beautiful.

*The storyteller paused. The children looked around and pondered. The storyteller went on:*

When the Everglades was perfect, people who called themselves Calusas arrived. They lived gracefully on the fish and game and made tools out of seashells.

The Spanish conquistadors arrived, and the Calusa people disappeared.

The conquistadors were afraid of the flesh-ripping grass and roaring animals of the Everglades, and they moved on.

North of Florida, European men pushed the Creek Indians out of the Carolinas. Some of them walked south until they came to the silvery Everglades. They poled deep

into the saw grass and settled on the islands. They are the Seminole Indians. A few of them live here today.

The storyteller paused. The children looked around.

"Where are the clouds of egrets?" a child asked.

The hunters shot them by the tens of thousands and sold the feathers to decorate women's hats. Only a few survived the slaughter.

"Where are the quantities of alligators?" another child asked.

The hunters shot them by the acres and sold

their gleaming hides to make wallets and shoes. Only a few remain.

"Where did the cathedral windows of orchids go?" a third child asked.

The orchid hunters picked gardens and gardens of them and sold them to put on ladies' dresses. Practically none can be found.

Another child looked around. "And where did the mammals and snails and one-celled plants and animals go?"

They vanished when the engineers dug canals in the Everglades and drained the

fresh water into the sea to make land. Farmers tilled the land; businesspeople built towns and roads upon it. Pesticides and fertilizers flowed into the river waters and poisoned the one-celled animals and plants. The snails died, the fish died, the mammals and birds died.

"But this is a sad story," said a fifth child. "Please tell us a happy story."

The storyteller picked up his pole and quietly skimmed the dugout canoe across the water and down a trail in the saw grass. Then he sat down and told the children a new story.

Five children and a storyteller poled into the Everglades.

Eventually the children grew up and ran the Earth.

The clouds of birds returned to an abundance of fish in the water. The flowers tumbled into bloom. Quantities of alligators bellowed through the saw grass again. A multitude of panthers, deer, raccoons, and otters cavorted on the islands.

"That's a much better story," said the children. "Now pole us home quickly so we can grow up."

# SYMBOLS OF THE VANISHING EVERGLADES

Green Anole

Swamp Lily

Deer Figurehead, created by Calusa Indians

Lightning Whelk

Great Egret

Tropical Zebra Butterfly

Calopogon Orchid

Florida Chicken Turtle

Liguus Tree Snail

Green Tree Frog

Brown Pelican

Everglades.    Text copyright © 1995 by Jean Craighead George.    Illustrations copyright © 1995 by Wendell Minor.    Printed in the U.S.A.
All rights reserved.    Library of Congress Cataloging-in-Publication Data    George, Jean Craighead, date.    Everglades / Jean Craighead George ;
paintings by Wendell Minor.    p.    cm.    Summary: Describes the Florida Everglades, the evolution of this unique area, and the impact
humans have had on its once-abundant life forms.    ISBN 0-06-021228-4. — ISBN 0-06-021229-2 (lib. bdg.). — ISBN 0-06-446194-7 (pbk.)
1. Everglades (Fla.)—Juvenile literature.    2. Everglades National Park (Fla.)—Juvenile literature.    [1. Everglades (Fla.)    2. Natural history—
Florida—Everglades.    3. Man—Influence on nature.]    I. Minor, Wendell, ill.    II. Title.    F317.E9G3    1995    975.9'39—dc20    92-9517
CIP    AC    Designed by Wendell Minor